The Unfinished Revolution

Davidson Omondi

Published by Davidson Omondi, 2025.

THE UNFINISHED REVOLUTION

First edition. August 14, 2025.

ISBN: 979-8231539130

Written by Davidson Omondi.

When you empower a woman, you ignite the potential of a nation

The Unfinished Revolution

How Empowering Africa's Women Will Unlock the World's Next Superpower

Dedication

To my first believers and my constant allies:

My mother, Benter Apiyo, and my father, Paul Kowino.

You laid the foundation upon which everything is built.

My siblings, Stephen, Elvince, Nelson, and Mary Faith.

My pillars of support in every revolution, big and small.

And to the sparks of the future,

The members of the Rongo University Gender Club (2025/2026 academic year).

May you be the ones to finish the work.

Foreword

This book is a powerful, insightful and a must read

Benter A. Omondi

Preface

There was a time when my father was down, and my mother, Benter Apiyo, had to become a man.

That is the only way I can describe it. In our community, the role of provider, of leader, of the unshakable pillar was a role reserved for a man. But when crisis struck our family, it was my mother who stepped into that space. She did not flinch. With the steel in her spine that I would later recognize as the quiet strength of millions of women, she fought to hold our world together. She worked, she planned, she strategized, and she carried the weight of our future on her shoulders.

I watched her do the work of two parents, with the ambition and vision of a seasoned CEO. But the world did not see a leader. It saw a woman standing in a man's shoes, and it judged her for it.

I saw it in the eyes of the loan officer who denied her the capital to expand her small business, the one she needed to secure our family's finances. I heard it in the dismissive tones of suppliers who would have treated a man with deference. I felt it in the opportunities that evaporated the moment they realized there was no man standing behind her. Her skill was never in question. Her work ethic was undeniable. Her vision was clear. But her gender was a barrier she could not overcome, a silent, unyielding wall.

It was in watching her struggle that the central question of this book was born. Why? Why was my mother's fierce capability not enough? Why did a system, built on the ghosts of patriarchy, refuse to acknowledge the power standing right in front of it?

This book is my answer. It began as a son's quiet observation of his mother's righteous struggle. It was forged in the passionate debates of the Rongo University Gender Club, where I learned that my mother's story was not hers alone, but the story of a continent. It was sharpened by years of research that gave data and language to the injustices I had witnessed with my own eyes.

I did not write this book to simply tell a sad story. I wrote it as an act of defiance. I wrote it to expose the invisible architecture of prejudice that holds back our mothers, our sisters, and our daughters. I wrote it to provide a blueprint for a world that does not force a woman to "become a man" to be seen as powerful, but one that recognizes and celebrates the unique, immense power she holds simply by being a woman.

This is for my mother, Benter, and for every woman who has ever been denied an opportunity not because she was incapable, but because she was a woman in a world that was not yet ready for her strength.

This is for my father, Paul, and for all the men who have seen the strength of the women beside them and know the world is better for it.

This is my part in the unfinished revolution.

Introduction: The Trillion-Dollar Question

In the tech hubs of Kigali and the agricultural heartlands of the Rift Valley, an economic revolution is taking place. It is not being driven by foreign investment or new commodities alone, but by the continent's most undervalued, most resilient, and most potent asset: its women. For every woman who shatters a glass ceiling, who builds a global brand from a single workshop, who ensures her daughters get the education she was denied, a spark is lit. These sparks, multiplied by millions, have the power to ignite Africa's ascent as the next global economic superpower.

Yet, this revolution is dangerously incomplete. For every celebrated success story, there are thousands more held back by invisible chains and concrete barriers we only pretend to have dismantled.

We talk about gender equality. For decades, the words have echoed in the halls of the United Nations and filled the pages of national policy documents. We sign global agreements like the Sustainable Development Goals (SDGs) and praise their ambition, particularly Goal 5, which stands as a global commitment to "Achieve gender equality and empower all women and girls." But for millions of women and girls across the continent, from the arid plains of the Sahel to the vibrant cities of the Cape, that promise remains an illusion, a ghost in a machine built by and for men.

The data is stark. The World Economic Forum's 2023 Global Gender Gap Report estimates that at the current pace, it will take 131 years to reach full parity globally. Sub-Saharan Africa, despite making significant progress, still has a gap of 32% to close. In the two arenas that matter most for a nation's prosperity—the classroom and the marketplace—this gap translates into a chasm of lost opportunity. This is not a failure of ambition, but a failure of action. It is a failure to see that gender equality is not a charitable side project or a matter of political correctness. It is the central economic and social issue of our time.

This book is a journey to the front lines of that struggle and a blueprint for a better, more prosperous future. We will move beyond the comfortable rhetoric and into the real, messy, and inspiring world of African women. We will meet the entrepreneurs who defied the odds, the innovators who navigate a system that often seems designed to make them fail. We will confront the hard truths within our education systems, where a girl's potential is still too often extinguished by early marriage, the long walk to a dilapidated school, or a curriculum that teaches her she is second-best.

But this is not another book that simply diagnoses the problem. This is a book about solutions. Grounded in a decade of research, on-the-ground case studies from the economic powerhouses of Kenya and South Africa to the rising stars across the continent, and a deep analysis of what truly works, this book offers tangible strategies. It is a call to action for policymakers, a guide for entrepreneurs, an essential text for educators, and a wake-up call for a world that has underestimated Africa's women for far too long.

By emphasizing the profound interconnectedness of the SDGs, we will illustrate how progress in gender equality (SDG 5) is the critical catalyst for achieving Quality Education (SDG 4), Decent Work and Economic Growth (SDG 8), and Reduced Inequalities (SDG 10). Unlocking the potential of half the population is not just about fairness; it is the single most powerful and pragmatic strategy for realizing the goals of the Africa Union's Agenda 2063 and building a future of inclusive, sustainable development for the entire continent.

The intended audience for this book is you. Whether you are a student, an educator, an entrepreneur, a policymaker, or simply a global citizen interested in the future of our world, this book is designed to provide valuable insights and practical recommendations. It aims to foster informed decision-making and, more importantly, to inspire effective action.

The question is no longer if we should act, but how—and how quickly. The cost of inaction is measured in trillions of dollars of lost GDP, in millions of stifled innovations, and in the immeasurable price of human potential left unfulfilled. The revolution has begun. This book is the manual for how we finish it.

Part I: The Anatomy of Inequality

Chapter 1: The Ghosts of History: How Colonialism Broke the Balance

To understand the inequality that persists in Africa today, we cannot simply look at the present. We must become historical detectives, tracing the origins of a system that was not accidentally, but deliberately, broken. The popular Western narrative is one of a continent historically steeped in patriarchy, with colonialism arriving as a complicated but modernizing force. This narrative is not only wrong; it is an inversion of the truth. In many parts of pre-colonial Africa, women held positions of immense power and influence that were systematically dismantled by a colonial project that imposed its own rigid, Victorian-era patriarchy as the law of the land.

The World Before: A Mosaic of Power

Before the Scramble for Africa, gender roles across the continent were a complex mosaic, but rarely did they conform to the simplistic patriarchal model of Europe. Power was often shared, and women's domains were sources of significant authority.

In the Ashanti Empire of modern-day Ghana, the society was matrilineal. The most powerful figure alongside the King (Asantehene) was the Queen Mother (Asantehemaa). She was no mere figurehead; she was the keeper of the royal lineage, a key political advisor, a judge in certain disputes, and held the unique power to nominate or veto the choice of the next king. Her influence was woven into the very fabric of governance. In the Kingdom of Dahomey, now Benin, this power took a martial form. The Agoji, or the "Dahomey Amazons," were an all-female military regiment of thousands of soldiers. They were elite frontline troops, feared for their ferocity, who played a crucial role in the kingdom's military expansion.

In the Igbo society of southeastern Nigeria, a system of dual-sex governance existed. While men's councils handled certain community affairs, women's councils (Umuada) held significant sway over markets, moral conduct, and issues affecting women. They could impose fines and boycotts, demonstrating a collective political and economic power that could check male authority. Among the Kikuyu of Kenya, women were the primary agriculturalists. While men cleared the land, women controlled its cultivation and the distribution of food, giving them fundamental control over the family's sustenance and economic well-being.

This is not to romanticize the pre-colonial era as a gender utopia. Patriarchal practices existed, and societies varied greatly. However, the crucial point is that structures existed that granted women economic autonomy, political voice, and spiritual authority. It was these very structures that colonialism identified as a threat to its model of control and systematically erased.

The Colonial Disruption: Imposing a Patriarchal Order

The arrival of European colonial powers in the late 19th century triggered a seismic and deliberate reordering of gender relations. The colonizers—whether British, French, Portuguese, or Belgian—brought with them their own deeply ingrained patriarchal ideologies and imposed them through law, economics, and religion.

The first and most devastating casualty was women's economic independence. Colonial administrators introduced cash-crop economies focused on products like coffee, cocoa, and cotton for export to Europe. These enterprises were almost exclusively placed in the hands of men. Men were taught new farming techniques and given access to seeds. Crucially, the colonial states passed laws formalizing land ownership in the name of individual men, ignoring traditional communal or female-centric land rights. The British in Kenya, through legislation like the Native Lands Registration Ordinance of 1959, systematically registered land to male heads of households, dispossessing women of their traditional rights to use and control land. This single act created generations of female economic dependency.

The second disruption was in education and politics. Colonial schools were established primarily to train a local cadre of male clerks, administrators, and soldiers to help run the colonial state. Boys were taught to read, write, and participate in the new cash economy. Girls, for the most part, were left behind or steered towards domestic science, creating an education and literacy gap that had not previously existed in such a stark form. Political power was similarly consolidated. The nuanced systems of shared governance were ignored. The British policy of "Indirect Rule" preferred to deal with a single male "chief" or "warrant chief," whom they could more easily control, thereby sidelining female voices from public life.

In South Africa, this process was amplified by the brutal system of apartheid. The government's policies were designed not just for racial segregation, but for total economic control. Pass laws, which severely restricted the movement of Black South Africans, were applied with particular harshness to women, tethering them to impoverished rural "homelands." The system was designed to make women dependent on the remittances of their husbands working in the mines, entrenching a migrant labor system that shattered families and destroyed women's economic autonomy.

After Independence: A New Fight on an Old Battlefield

The wave of independence movements that swept across Africa in the mid-20th century was a moment of immense hope, and women were at the heart of the struggle. In Algeria's war for independence, women served as fighters and intelligence agents. In South Africa, the 1956 Women's March on the Union Buildings in Pretoria, where 20,000 women protested the pass laws, was a landmark event. Women like Albertina Sisulu and Winnie Madikizela-Mandela became icons of the movement.

This activism created a powerful foundation. As new nations were born, many enshrined gender equality in their new constitutions. Kenya's 2010 constitution is a prime example, making gender equality a fundamental right and mandating the famous "two-thirds gender rule." In post-apartheid South Africa, the 1996 Constitution became one of the most progressive in the world, explicitly forbidding discrimination on the basis of gender, sex, and sexual orientation.

Yet, despite these legal milestones, the colonial legacy of patriarchy has proven stubbornly persistent. Laws written on paper are not always reflected in the reality of daily life. The economic structures that favor men are deeply entrenched. The fight for gender equality in modern Africa is not a new fight. It is the continuation of a struggle against a system that was deliberately broken, a fight to reclaim the power that was lost and to build a future where the equality promised in constitutions is a lived reality for every woman and girl.

Chapter 2: The Data That Defines a Continent: Mapping the Modern Gender Gap

Words like "disparity" and "inequality" can feel abstract. To grasp the true scale of the challenge and the opportunity, we must turn to the data. Statistics are not just numbers; they are the stories of girls who leave school too early, of women who die in childbirth from preventable causes, of brilliant entrepreneurs who cannot secure a loan, and of citizens who cannot access the digital world. When we map this data across Africa, a clear and often startling picture emerges. It is a picture of incredible progress mixed with profound and persistent gaps that hold the entire continent back.

The Education Story: The Leaky Pipeline

On the surface, the story of education in Africa is a triumph. Thanks to global initiatives and dedicated national policies, the gender gap in primary school has all but vanished in many countries. This is a monumental achievement. But this encouraging picture hides a more troubling reality. The educational journey is a pipeline, and across the continent, that pipeline is leaky—and it leaks girls at a much faster rate than boys.

In Kenya, while primary enrolment is near parity, the Gross Enrolment Ratio (GER) for secondary school reveals a gap: in 2022, it was approximately 72% for boys but only 65% for girls. This seven-point difference represents tens of thousands of lost dreams. In more fragile states like Chad, the gap is a chasm, with secondary enrolment rates for girls being less than half that of boys.

South Africa presents a different paradox. Here, women have actually overtaken men in tertiary enrolment. More women than men are attending university. However, a closer look reveals "horizontal segregation." Women are overwhelmingly concentrated in fields like education and social sciences. In the high-paying fields of Science, Technology, Engineering, and Mathematics (STEM), men still dominate. According to UNESCO, across Sub-Saharan Africa, women make up only about 30% of students in STEM fields.

The Health and Survival Story: A Matter of Life and Death

Gender inequality is not just about opportunity; it's about life and death. Sub-Saharan Africa has the highest maternal mortality rates in the world. A woman in the region has a 1 in 37 lifetime risk of dying during pregnancy or childbirth. In a high-income country, that risk is 1 in 4,900. This is not a medical problem; it is a gender problem. It reflects women's lack of access to basic healthcare, family planning services, and education.

Furthermore, HIV/AIDS disproportionately affects women and girls. Young women in Africa are more than twice as likely to be living with HIV as their male peers. This is driven by a combination of biological vulnerability, lack of access to education, and harmful gender norms that limit their power to negotiate safe sex.

The Economic Story: Unequal Work, Unequal Pay, Unseen Labor

Across Sub-Saharan Africa, women's labor force participation rate hovers around 61%, compared to 72% for men. This doesn't tell the whole story. Women are far more likely to be in vulnerable employment—unpaid family work or informal, low-wage jobs with no security or benefits. The International Labour Organization estimates that over 74% of women in non-agricultural jobs in the region are in informal employment.

For those in the formal sector, a steep pay gap persists. Globally, women earn about 77 cents for every dollar a man earns. In many African countries, this gap is wider, particularly when comparing similar roles and education levels.

The biggest blind spot in our economic data is the crushing burden of unpaid care work. The UNDP reports that women in Africa spend up to 3.4 more hours a day on unpaid care work than men. This is the work of collecting water and firewood, cooking, cleaning, and caring for children and the elderly. It is essential, back-breaking labor that is completely absent from GDP calculations. It is time that cannot be spent on education, on earning an income, or on participating in public life.

The Digital and Legal Story: The New Frontier of Inequality

As economies digitize, a new gap has emerged. In Africa, the gender gap in mobile internet use is 28%, and women are 37% less likely than men to own a mobile phone. This digital divide prevents women from accessing information, financial services, and online markets, effectively locking them out of the 21st-century economy.

Legally, while many constitutions guarantee equality, discriminatory laws persist. A World Bank report, Women, Business and the Law 2023, found that Sub-Saharan Africa has made huge strides but still has an average score of just 72.5 out of 100 on the index of legal equality. In some countries, laws still restrict women's ability to get a job, register a business, or inherit property without the permission of a husband.

The numbers tell a clear, multi-faceted story. While Africa has made incredible strides, deep structural inequalities remain across every facet of life. These are not separate issues. A girl who is uneducated is more likely to face health complications, to be in vulnerable employment, and to be digitally excluded. Closing these gaps is the most urgent task facing the continent today.

Chapter 3: The Schoolhouse Ceiling: Education's Promise and Peril

Education should be the great equalizer, the silver bullet that breaks cycles of poverty. For many African girls, it is. But for far too many others, the schoolhouse is the site of a cruel double bind: even as it offers the promise of liberation, it simultaneously reinforces the very inequalities it is supposed to dismantle. The barriers are not just about getting girls to school; they are about what happens—and what doesn't happen—once they are inside the school gates, and the growing threats of conflict and climate change that can slam those gates shut.

Physical Barriers: The Long Walk to a Locked Door

The first hurdle is simply getting there. For millions of girls in rural Africa, the journey to school is a daily act of courage on unsafe roads. This journey exposes them to harassment and violence. Once they arrive, the facilities themselves can be a barrier. A shocking number of schools across the continent lack basic, gender-segregated toilets. For an adolescent girl, the lack of a clean, private, and safe place to manage her period is a primary reason to stay home. This "period poverty" forces countless girls to miss up to a week of school every month, creating an academic deficit from which it is nearly impossible to recover. Simple interventions, like the Kenyan government's program to provide free sanitary pads, have proven to be game-changers.

The cost of education, even when tuition is free, is another locked door. The price of uniforms, books, and exam fees can be prohibitive. When resources are scarce, a deeply ingrained cultural bias often leads families to prioritize a son's education. A boy's education is seen as an investment; a girl's is often viewed as a temporary expense before she is married off to another family.

Pedagogical Barriers: The Hidden Curriculum of Silence

For the girls who overcome these physical barriers, a more subtle form of inequality awaits them in the classroom. This is the "hidden curriculum"—the unstated lessons, values, and perspectives that students absorb. Curricula and textbooks across the continent are often riddled with gender stereotypes. Men are depicted as doctors, engineers, and presidents. Women, if they appear at all, are shown as mothers, nurses, or market vendors. The contributions of powerful historical women are erased.

This sends a powerful message: leadership and innovation are male attributes. This is particularly damaging in STEM fields. Teachers, often overworked and unconsciously biased, may call on boys more, praise them for being "assertive" while chiding girls for the same behavior by calling them "bossy." This quietly suffocates a girl's ambition within the very walls that were meant to nurture it.

Cultural and Safety Barriers: The Culture of Fear

The most insidious barrier is the culture of fear created by School-Related Gender-Based Violence (SRGBV). Schools should be safe havens, but for too many girls, they are places of risk from both fellow students and teachers. The crisis of GBV on South African university campuses is well-documented, but the problem starts much earlier. When a girl is assaulted, the system often fails her. She may be blamed, ostracized, or forced to drop out due to pregnancy.

This is compounded by the societal pressure of early marriage. Each year, according to UNICEF, about 12 million girls under 18 are married. In Sub-Saharan Africa, 4 in 10 young women were married as children. A family living in poverty may see marrying their daughter off as one less mouth to feed. Her education is seen as secondary to her role as a future wife.

Emerging Threats: Climate and Conflict

Two powerful forces are threatening to reverse decades of progress in girls' education: climate change and conflict.

As climate change brings more frequent and severe droughts and floods, it is girls who are often the first to be pulled out of school. They are needed at home to spend more hours fetching water from distant sources or to help the family survive. A Malala Fund report estimated that by 2025, climate-related events could prevent at least 12.5 million girls from completing their education each year.

In conflict zones, schools are often targets, and girls are uniquely vulnerable to abduction and exploitation by armed groups, as tragically demonstrated by the Boko Haram kidnappings in Nigeria. Displacement forces families from their homes, and in the chaos of refugee camps, girls' education is rarely a priority.

This is the double bind. The school system holds the key to a girl's future, but it is a system rife with physical, pedagogical, and cultural barriers. To unlock Africa's potential, we must do more than just build schools. We must fundamentally redesign them into true sanctuaries of safety and engines of genuine equality, resilient enough to withstand the gathering storms of our time.

Part II: The Price of Exclusion

Chapter 4: The $42 Billion Lockbox: Capital, Collateral, and the 'Boys' Club'

If education is the first battleground for gender equality, then entrepreneurship is the second. Africa is a continent of entrepreneurs. Women are at the very heart of this energy, starting new ventures at a higher rate than men. They are, by necessity and by nature, resilient and creative. And yet, when it comes to scaling a business—to moving from a market stall to a factory—women run into a wall. This wall is guarded by gatekeepers who control the flow of capital and opportunity. The African Development Bank has quantified the size of this wall: it is a $42 billion financing gap for women entrepreneurs. This is the lockbox holding back the continent's growth.

The Collateral Trap and the Bias of Bankers

The first key to the lockbox is capital, and the first barrier is the demand for collateral. Decades of discriminatory inheritance laws mean that property and land—the forms of collateral most prized by traditional banks—are overwhelmingly owned by men. Without collateral, the doors of formal banking are often slammed shut.

But even a woman with collateral faces the hurdle of implicit bias. Loan officers, who are predominantly male, are more likely to perceive a woman's business as a risky "hobby" or a small-scale "side project," while viewing a man's identical venture as a serious "investment." Research has shown they ask women different types of questions—"prevention-focused" questions about how they will avoid losing money, while asking men "promotion-focused" questions about their vision for growth. This framing difference has a huge impact on funding outcomes.

The Vast, Vital, and Vulnerable Informal Economy

The majority of Africa's women entrepreneurs operate in the informal economy. This sector, which accounts for over 85% of total employment in Africa, is the lifeblood of the continent. It is where women run market stalls, provide tailoring services, and operate small-scale food businesses. This work is vital, providing essential goods and services and income for millions of families.

However, informality is a double-edged sword. It means these businesses are not registered, pay no taxes, and have no legal standing. This makes them invisible to policymakers and, crucially, to formal lenders. It also means they operate without a safety net. There is no social security, no health insurance, and no legal protection. A woman in the informal sector is one illness or one market fire away from losing everything. The struggle to formalize a business—a process that can be bureaucratic, expensive, and intimidating—is a major barrier keeping women trapped in this cycle of vulnerability.

The Unspoken Rules of the 'Boys' Club'

Capital is not the only resource controlled by gatekeepers. Just as important are the networks that provide access to information, mentorship, and high-value contracts. In many sectors, the most important decisions are not made in the boardroom; they are made on the golf course, over drinks after work, or within alumni associations from elite all-boys schools. These are the informal networks of the "boys' club."

A woman in the construction industry may be the most qualified bidder for a government contract, but she may lose out to a less-qualified male competitor who happens to play golf with the minister. A female tech founder won't even hear about a crucial meeting with venture capitalists because it was organized through a private WhatsApp group of male founders. This exclusion is often not malicious. It's the product of affinity bias—people naturally gravitate towards and trust others who are like them.

Mentorship is a critical component of this. But male leaders are more likely to mentor younger men who remind them of themselves. This leaves aspiring women entrepreneurs without the guidance they need to scale the steep learning curve of business growth.

The Crushing Weight of the Double Shift

The final barrier is a fundamental societal imbalance. Women are expected to be full-time entrepreneurs and full-time caregivers. The "double shift"—running a business all day and then coming home to manage all the unpaid care work—is a crushing weight. It is time that cannot be spent on networking or strategic planning. Male entrepreneurs are far more likely to have a spouse at home managing the domestic sphere, freeing them to focus entirely on their business. Female entrepreneurs rarely have this luxury.

These barriers—a lack of capital and collateral, the trap of informality, exclusion from powerful networks, and the societal expectation of the double shift—create a formidable obstacle course. It forces women to be more creative and more resilient just to stay in the game. Imagine how much faster Africa's economies would grow if we simply cleared the path and opened the lockbox.

Chapter 5: The Lionesses: Real Stories of Women Who Built Empires

Despite the systemic barriers, women across Africa are not just surviving in business; they are building empires. They are rewriting the rules of technology, manufacturing, and agriculture. Their stories are not just inspiring; they are a masterclass in resilience and innovation. To understand the future of African business, we must learn from the lionesses who are building it today.

The Tech Pioneer: Rebecca Enonchong, Cameroon

Rebecca Enonchong is one of Africa's most respected tech entrepreneurs. Born in Cameroon, she moved to the US as a teenager, where she studied and began her career. In 1999, at a time when the dominant narrative about Africa was one of poverty and aid, she founded AppsTech, a global provider of enterprise software solutions. She built a world-class tech company serving clients like the World Bank and Halliburton, not from Silicon Valley, but with a back office in her home country. Her model was revolutionary: provide high-end tech services from Africa to the world.

Her journey was fraught with challenges. She faced skepticism from clients who couldn't believe a company operating from Cameroon could deliver complex software solutions. She navigated the immense infrastructural challenges of the time, from unreliable internet to power outages. But her biggest contribution may be her work building the continent's tech ecosystem. She is the founder of the African Business Angel Network (ABAN) and ActivSpaces, a tech hub in Cameroon that provides resources and mentorship to young entrepreneurs. Rebecca Enonchong didn't just build a company; she helped build an entire industry, proving that African tech could compete at the highest level.

The Brewer Who Broke a Monopoly: Tabitha Karanja, Kenya

In 1997, Tabitha Karanja and her husband saw a gap in Kenya's alcoholic beverage market. The industry was dominated by a single, powerful multinational, East African Breweries Limited (EABL). The local offerings for the lower end of the market were often illicit and dangerous. The Karanjas decided to start a fortified wine business, but soon realized the real opportunity was in beer. In 2008, they launched Summit Lager, the first beer brewed by a locally-owned company in Kenya in decades. This was the birth of Keroche Breweries.

The battle that followed was epic. Keroche faced intense competition, regulatory hurdles that seemed designed to protect the incumbent, and crippling tax demands that nearly shut them down on multiple occasions. Tabitha Karanja became a household name in Kenya, a symbol of local resilience against a corporate giant. She fought her battles in the courts and in the media, framing the struggle as one of David versus Goliath, of Kenyan enterprise against foreign domination. Today, Keroche Breweries is a multi-billion shilling company and the second-largest brewer in the country. Tabitha's story is a powerful testament to the sheer tenacity required to break into an established, male-dominated industry.

The Footwear Revolutionary: Bethlehem Tilahun Alemu, Ethiopia

Bethlehem Tilahun Alemu grew up in Zenabwork, a poor community in Addis Ababa, Ethiopia. She saw the immense talent of the local artisans around her, who could create beautiful products but had no way to access a global market. In 2005, with a small loan from her family, she founded soleRebels. Her idea was both simple and brilliant: create world-class footwear based on traditional Ethiopian designs—like the famous "barabasso" tire-soled shoes—and sell them to the world as a premium, eco-friendly brand.

SoleRebels was founded on principles of sustainability and fair trade long before they became global buzzwords. The shoes are made from locally sourced, recycled, and organic materials. The company is the world's first to be certified by the World Fair Trade Organization (WFTO). Her employees receive salaries that are three to four times the industry average, along with full medical benefits. From a workshop on her grandmother's land, Bethlehem has built soleRebels into one of the world's fastest-growing footwear brands, with standalone stores in the US, Europe, and Asia. She has redefined what "Made in Africa" means, transforming it from a symbol of charity to a mark of world-class craftsmanship and cutting-edge style.

These are just three of the thousands of lionesses rewriting Africa's economic story. They faced down bias, broke monopolies, and built global brands from the ground up. They did not wait for the system to change; they changed it themselves. Their success is living proof of the immense, untapped power that is just waiting to be fully unleashed across the African continent.

Chapter 6: The Uncalculated Trillion: The Hard Economics of Empowerment

For too long, the conversation around gender equality has been confined to the language of human rights and social justice. These are the most important reasons to pursue it. But in the halls of government and the boardrooms of corporations, decisions are often made based on a different language: the language of economics. To accelerate the unfinished revolution, we must become fluent in this language. We must make the business case for gender equality so clear that ignoring it becomes an act of economic malpractice. Empowerment is not a cost center; it is the single greatest growth opportunity in the world today.

The Trillion-Dollar Prize

Leading economic institutions have quantified the cost of gender inequality, and the numbers are staggering. A landmark study by the McKinsey Global Institute found that if women were to participate in the economy identically to men, it would add as much as $28 trillion to the world's annual GDP by 2025.

For Africa, the potential prize is transformative. The United Nations Development Programme (UNDP) calculates that gender inequality is costing Sub-Saharan Africa, on average, $95 billion a year in lost economic potential, peaking at $105 billion in 2014. This is not a small rounding error. It is more than double the total international aid received by the region. We are not talking about finding new money. We are talking about unlocking the wealth that is already there, latent in the potential of the continent's women.

This loss comes from the leaky pipeline in education. It comes from the employment gap. And it comes from the gender pay gap.

Unlocking the Demographic Dividend

Many African nations have a huge potential advantage: a youth bulge. A large population of young people can lead to a "demographic dividend," a period of accelerated economic growth driven by an expanding workforce. However, this dividend is not automatic. It can only be realized if the young population is healthy, educated, and productively employed.

Gender equality is the key that unlocks this dividend. When girls are educated, they tend to marry later and have fewer, healthier children. This slows population growth and reduces dependency ratios. When women are empowered to join the workforce, the labor pool doubles, and household incomes rise, creating a virtuous cycle of saving and investment. A country that fails to educate its girls and empower its women will miss its demographic window, and a youth bulge can quickly turn from a potential dividend into a source of social instability.

The Alpha of Female Leadership

The business case extends into the corporate world itself. A mountain of evidence shows that companies with more women in leadership are more profitable, more innovative, and have better governance. The Peterson Institute for International Economics, in a study of nearly 22,000 firms in 91 countries, found that a company with 30 percent female leadership could expect to add up to 6 percentage points to its net margin compared to a similar business with no female leaders.

Why? Diverse teams make better decisions. They are less prone to groupthink and better at problem-solving. Women leaders are often associated with better corporate social responsibility and are more attuned to the needs of a diverse customer base. In Africa, where companies need to be incredibly innovative and resilient to succeed, ignoring this "diversity alpha" is a critical error.

Stability, Security, and Growth

Finally, there is a powerful link between gender equality and national stability. Research from organizations like the Council on Foreign Relations has shown that the security of women is a critical indicator of the security of the state. Countries where women are less equal are more likely to be involved in conflict and to be less stable. Conversely, when women are involved in peace negotiations, the resulting agreements are 35% more likely to last at least 15 years. Investing in women's empowerment is not just a development strategy; it is a security strategy.

Making the economic case is crucial because it shifts the framing of the issue. Gender equality is no longer a "special interest" topic but a central pillar of national economic and security strategy. It transforms a minister of gender affairs from a marginalized cabinet member to a key partner of the minister of finance. It gives business leaders a powerful, bottom-line reason to change their practices. It provides a clear, data-driven answer to the question, "Why should we invest in women?" The answer is simple: because it is the most intelligent investment we can make in our shared future.

Part III: The Blueprint for a Revolution

Chapter 7: Allies and Advocates: The Essential Role of Men

The struggle for gender equality cannot be won by women alone. It is not a "women's issue"; it is a human issue. The patriarchal systems that hold women back also impose rigid and often harmful expectations on men, confining them to narrow definitions of masculinity. To dismantle this system, we need men to move beyond passive support and become active allies and vocal advocates. This is not about men "saving" women; it is about men recognizing their shared interest in a more equal world and taking responsibility for changing the status quo.

From Bystander to Upstander

For too long, the dominant role for men in conversations about gender has been one of silence. A sexist joke in the office, a colleague being interrupted in a meeting, a discriminatory policy—these are moments where silence is complicity. An ally is someone who is willing to move from being a bystander to being an "upstander."

This means actively speaking out. It's the male manager who says, "Let her finish her point," when a female colleague is interrupted. It's the man who refuses to laugh at a sexist joke and explains why it's not funny. It's the father who challenges the school's assumption that his wife will be the primary contact for their children's needs. These small, daily acts of courage are what begin to shift a culture.

Organizations across Africa are beginning to focus on engaging men. In South Africa, groups like Sonke Gender Justice work with men and boys to challenge patriarchal norms and combat gender-based violence. They recognize that violence against women is not a women's problem, but a men's problem. Their programs create safe spaces for men to discuss toxic masculinity, fatherhood, and healthy relationships, fostering a new generation of men who see gender equality as a source of strength, not a threat.

Challenging the "Man Box"

The pressure on men to conform to traditional masculinity—to be tough, unemotional, dominant, and the sole breadwinner—is immense. This "man box" is not only limiting for men's own emotional well-being, leading to higher rates of suicide and stress-related illness, but it is also a primary driver of inequality. A man who feels his identity is threatened by his wife earning more than him is less likely to support her career. A man who believes showing emotion is a sign of weakness is less likely to be an engaged and nurturing father.

Promoting gender equality frees men from this box. When caregiving is seen as a shared responsibility, men are liberated to build deeper bonds with their children. When a woman's income is valued, it reduces the immense pressure on a man to be the sole provider. An equal partnership is a stronger, more resilient partnership, better able to withstand life's economic and emotional shocks.

Men as Agents of Change in Institutions

The most powerful role for male allies is within the institutions where they hold the majority of power. Male leaders are the gatekeepers who can open the doors to change.

This means a male CEO must do more than just say he supports diversity; he must actively sponsor high-potential women, ensuring they get the challenging assignments and visibility needed for promotion. He must demand diverse slates of candidates for every senior role. He must hold his leadership team accountable for hitting gender parity targets with the same rigor he applies to financial targets.

It means male politicians must use their influence to champion laws that advance gender equality, from equal property rights to paid parental leave for both parents. It means male community elders must publicly condemn harmful traditional practices like FGM and child marriage and advocate for girls' education.

The call for men to become allies is not an accusation; it is an invitation. It is an invitation to share the burden and the benefits of building a more just world. The revolution will only be complete when men and women are fighting side-by-side, not as opposing forces, but as equal partners in a shared human project.

Chapter 8: Leapfrogging with Laptops: Technology as a Double-Edged Sword

Technology is Africa's great accelerator. The mobile phone revolution has transformed the continent over the past two decades, leapfrogging the need for landlines and connecting millions to information and finance for the first time. For women, technology offers a powerful pathway to empowerment, a tool to bypass traditional gatekeepers and access education, markets, and capital. However, technology is not a neutral force. It is a double-edged sword that, without deliberate action, can also amplify existing inequalities and create new ones.

The Promise: Digital Doors to Opportunity

The power of technology to empower women is undeniable. Consider the impact of mobile money. Services like Kenya's M-Pesa have been revolutionary for female entrepreneurs. For the first time, a woman running a market stall could securely save small amounts of money, receive payments from customers, and build a transaction history on her phone—all without needing a traditional bank account. This has been a critical first step towards financial inclusion for millions.

In education, online platforms offer access to world-class learning resources for girls who may be unable to attend a physical school. Telemedicine can provide rural women with access to vital health advice, bypassing the need to travel long distances to a clinic. E-commerce platforms allow female artisans to sell their products directly to a global market, cutting out the middlemen who once took most of their profits. Social media has given women a powerful tool to organize, advocate for their rights, and hold leaders accountable, as seen in movements like Nigeria's #EndSARS protests, where women were key organizers.

Technology can directly address some of the key barriers women face. It can bring the bank, the market, and the classroom to a woman's fingertips, reducing the constraints of her limited mobility and the burden of the double shift.

The Peril: The Deepening Digital Divide

The greatest danger is that the benefits of technology will not be shared equally. As discussed earlier, there is a significant gender gap in access to technology across Africa. Women are less likely to own a smartphone and less likely to use mobile internet than men. This "digital divide" is driven by several factors.

First, cost. A smartphone and a data plan are expensive, and when a family's resources are limited, the son is often prioritized. Second, digital literacy. The historical gap in education means women, particularly in older generations, are less likely to have the skills and confidence to use digital technology. Third, the availability of relevant content. Much of the content online is not created by or for African women, making it less useful or engaging for them.

This divide matters immensely. As more essential services—from government registration to job applications to banking—move online, women who are digitally excluded risk being locked out of the modern economy and public life entirely.

The Threat: Online Harassment and Algorithmic Bias

Beyond access, there is the issue of safety. The internet can be a hostile environment for women. Online harassment, hate speech, and the non-consensual sharing of intimate images are rampant and used to silence women's voices. The anonymity of the internet often emboldens perpetrators, and legal frameworks have been slow to catch up. For a woman considering entering public life or becoming a vocal advocate, the threat of online abuse is a powerful deterrent.

Furthermore, the algorithms that shape our digital world can perpetuate and even amplify real-world biases. An algorithm designed to screen job applications might learn from historical data that men are more likely to be hired for leadership roles and therefore start to automatically downgrade female candidates. A loan application assessed by an AI might unfairly penalize a woman for having a thinner credit file, ignoring the systemic reasons for that difference. If we are not careful, we risk building our past biases into the automated systems of the future.

Forging a Digital Future for All

To ensure technology is a force for equality, not division, we need a deliberate strategy. This means investing in programs that improve digital literacy for women and girls. It means promoting the creation of local, relevant content in local languages. It means designing financial products and digital platforms with the needs of female users at their core. Crucially, it means taking online gender-based violence seriously, creating strong laws and holding social media platforms accountable for the safety of their users.

The tech revolution is happening, with or without a gender strategy. The choice before us is whether we allow it to leave half the population behind, or whether we harness its immense power to accelerate the unfinished revolution and build a more equal future for all.

Chapter 9: The Proven Models: Scaling Success from the Ground Up

The problems of gender inequality are vast, but they are not unsolvable. Across Africa, pockets of the future are already being built. Trailblazing organizations and innovative governments are creating models that work. This is not a matter of theory; it is a matter of proven success. The challenge is not to invent solutions from scratch, but to identify, fund, and scale what is already working.

Education: The Holistic Approach of CAMFED

One of the most celebrated models in education is that of the Campaign for Female Education (CAMFED). Operating in several African countries, CAMFED's success lies in its comprehensive support system that recognizes a girl needs more than just school fees. They provide a full package: tuition, uniforms, books, and sanitary pads. They create a local support network of "teacher mentors" and community members who protect girls from exploitation.

But the true genius of the model is the Cama alumnae network. When a girl graduates, she joins a powerful network of over 250,000 young women. These graduates become leaders, entrepreneurs, and activists in their own right. Crucially, they use their own resources and influence to support the next generation of girls, becoming philanthropists themselves. This creates a virtuous, self-perpetuating cycle of empowerment. CAMFED has proven that when you invest in one girl's education, you are investing in the future of her entire community.

Financial Inclusion: The Village Savings and Loan Association (VSLA) Model

To bypass the biased formal banking system, one of the most powerful grassroots solutions has been the Village Savings and Loan Association (VSLA) model, championed by organizations like CARE and Oxfam. The concept is simple. A group of 15-25 self-selected individuals, usually women, meet regularly to save small, fixed amounts of money in a shared lockbox. As the fund grows, members can take out small loans, which are paid back with a small amount of interest, growing the group's capital.

There is no external capital; the system is entirely self-funded and self-managed. This model builds financial discipline, provides members with access to credit for emergencies or small business investments, and creates a powerful social safety net. It gives women experience in financial management and governance. For millions of women, a VSLA is their first step on the ladder of financial inclusion, a model that has been successfully replicated across the continent.

Legal Empowerment: The Paralegals of TIMAP for Justice

Access to justice is critical, but formal legal systems are often intimidating and expensive for poor women. In Sierra Leone, the organization TIMAP for Justice has pioneered a powerful model of community-based paralegals. They train local, trusted community members—not lawyers—in the basics of national law and alternative dispute resolution.

These paralegals become the first port of call for justice. A woman facing a land dispute or a case of domestic violence can go to her local paralegal for free, accessible advice. The paralegal can mediate the dispute, connect the woman with government services, or, if necessary, help her navigate the formal court system. This model demystifies the law and brings justice directly to the people who need it most, empowering women to understand and claim their rights.

Health: The Community Health Worker Model

To combat high maternal and child mortality, countries like Ethiopia and Rwanda have achieved stunning success by deploying massive networks of community health workers, the vast majority of whom are women. These workers are trained to provide basic health services right in their own villages. They visit pregnant women to provide prenatal advice, ensure children get their immunizations, provide family planning services, and teach families about nutrition and sanitation.

They are the bridge between the community and the formal health system. By bringing care to people's doorsteps, they overcome the barriers of distance and cost that prevent so many women from accessing clinics. Rwanda's use of community health workers was a key factor in reducing its maternal mortality rate by nearly 80% between 2000 and 2017. It is a powerful demonstration of how investing in female health workers can transform the health of an entire nation.

These are not pilot projects. They are proven, scalable solutions that address the core barriers women face in education, finance, law, and health. They show that change is possible when solutions are designed with the community, for the community. The blueprint for the revolution already exists. The task now is to roll it out.

Chapter 10: The Leader's Playbook: An Action Plan for Governments and Corporations

Change cannot be left to chance or goodwill alone. It requires deliberate, strategic, and courageous action from leaders at every level. This chapter is a playbook, a set of clear, evidence-based recommendations for those with the power to write the rules, allocate the resources, and shape the culture.

For National Governments: Rewriting the Rules of the Game

Legislate and Enforce Radical Equality:

Modernize the Law: Conduct a full review of all national laws—from property and inheritance statutes to family and commercial codes—to eliminate any gender discrimination. Abolish any law that requires a woman to get her husband's permission to get a passport, register a business, or get a job. Guarantee women's equal right to own and inherit land.

Enforce Quotas: The experiences of Rwanda and South Africa show that quotas work to break up the old boys' club. Enact and, crucially, enforce laws like Kenya's two-thirds gender rule for all elective and appointive bodies, including the judiciary and civil service.

Mandate Gender-Based Procurement: Mandate that a significant percentage (e.g., 30%) of all public procurement contracts be awarded to women-owned businesses. This uses the massive purchasing power of the state to build a new class of female entrepreneurs.

Follow the Money: Gender-Responsive Budgeting and the Care Economy:

Analyze the Budget: Implement Gender-Responsive Budgeting. This means analyzing the entire national budget to understand how it impacts men and women differently, and then adjusting allocations to close the gaps.

Invest in the Care Economy: Invest in public infrastructure that reduces the burden of unpaid care work: piped water, rural electrification, and, most importantly, affordable, high-quality public childcare. These are high-return economic investments.

Prioritize Safety and Justice:

Strengthen Laws Against GBV: Enact and enforce strong laws against domestic violence, sexual assault, and online harassment, with specialized police units and courts to handle these cases.

Fund Women's Shelters and Legal Aid: Provide significant public funding for shelters, crisis centers, and legal aid services for survivors of violence.

For the Private Sector: The Competitive Advantage of Equality

Measure, Report, and Act on the Data:

Conduct a Pay Audit: Conduct a transparent gender pay audit to identify and close wage gaps.

Set and Report on Targets: Set public targets for the representation of women at every level of seniority, from entry-level to the board. Tie executive bonuses to meeting these targets.

Redesign the System of Work:

Blind Recruitment and Structured Interviews: Use blind CVs and structured interviews to combat unconscious bias in hiring. Ensure promotion criteria are objective and transparent.

Implement Paid Parental Leave for All: Offer generous, paid parental leave for both mothers and fathers. This is one of the most powerful tools for normalizing shared caregiving.

Embrace Flexibility: Offer flexible working hours and remote work options. This helps both men and women balance work and family responsibilities.

Vote with Your Wallet and Your Platform:

Diversify the Supply Chain: Actively seek out and procure goods and services from women-owned businesses. Large corporations can create supplier diversity programs to facilitate this.

Use Your Voice: Use the company's platform and advertising power to challenge gender stereotypes and promote positive representations of women and girls.

For International Partners and Civil Society: Fueling the Revolution

Fund Women Directly: Shift funding models away from large, top-down projects towards direct, flexible, long-term support for local, women-led organizations and cooperatives.

Invest in What Works: Rigorously evaluate programs and channel significant funding towards scaling proven models like VSLAs and community paralegal services.

Advocate and Hold Accountable: Use international platforms to advocate for legal and policy reforms. Support independent media and civil society watchdogs that hold governments and corporations accountable for their commitments.

No single actor can finish this revolution alone. But with a clear playbook and the political will to act, these steps can transform the landscape of opportunity for Africa's women, and in doing so, unlock a new era of prosperity for all.

Conclusion: The Real Work Begins

We began this journey with a simple, powerful premise: that the empowerment of Africa's women is the single most important key to unlocking the continent's future as a global economic and social powerhouse. We have traveled through history, uncovering how systems of power were deliberately constructed to exclude women. We have mapped the stark data of the modern gender gap. We have heard the real stories of the lionesses who built empires against all odds. We have made the hard economic case, demonstrating that equality is not a matter of charity, but of trillions of dollars in potential wealth. And we have laid out a clear blueprint for action.

Now, we stand at a crossroads. The era of pilot projects must give way to an era of bold, systemic change. The unfinished revolution must be our generation's great work.

This is not a task for presidents and CEOs alone. It is a task for every one of us.

It is for the teacher who ensures he calls on the quiet girl in the back of the class. It is for the male entrepreneur who actively sponsors a high-potential female colleague. It is for the banker who champions new ways to get capital into the hands of women. It is for the father who takes parental leave and teaches his sons to respect women as their equals. It is for the woman who, having broken through a barrier, makes it her mission to hold the door open for those who come after her.

The forces of inertia and tradition are strong. The path ahead is not easy. But the cost of inaction is far greater than the cost of change. It is the cost of a continent operating at half-capacity. It is the cost of innovations we will never see, businesses that will never be built, and problems that will go unsolved. It is the moral and economic cost of telling half of our population that their dreams are less valid.

Imagine a young girl, somewhere on the continent, starting school today. Let us call her "Amani," the Swahili word for peace. Whether the world she graduates into is one of limited horizons or limitless possibility depends on the choices we make now. Will she be able to get a loan based on the brilliance of her idea, not the gender on her ID card? Will her voice be heard in the halls of power? Will she be able to build a life based on the full measure of her talent and ambition?

The answer to these questions will define the future of Africa. Let us choose to build a world where Amani's success is not the exception, but the rule. Let us choose to invest in her, to believe in her, and to clear the path for her. Let us choose to finish this revolution. The real work begins now.

Acknowledgments

No book, especially one that hopes to capture a revolution, is ever the work of a single person. This project is built on the generosity, wisdom, and support of a vast community of people to whom I owe a profound debt of gratitude.

My first and deepest thanks go to the women who shared their stories with me. Your courage to speak your truth, to recount moments of both struggle and triumph, is the heart and soul of this book. To those who allowed me to use their real names, and to those whose stories I told while protecting their identity, thank you for trusting me with your experiences. This book is a testament to your resilience.

I am also deeply indebted to the pioneering "Lionesses" of African business, Rebecca Enonchong, Tabitha Karanja, and Bethlehem Tilahun Alemu, whose publicly documented journeys provided a blueprint for what is possible and served as a powerful inspiration for this work.

This book was born and nurtured at Rongo University, my intellectual home. I am grateful for the environment of rigorous inquiry and debate it provided. A special thank you to the members and faculty advisor of the Rongo University Gender Club (2025/2026). Your passion, insights, and refusal to accept the status quo sharpened every argument in these pages. I am also grateful to the librarians and professors who guided my research and challenged my thinking.

To my family, who have lived this book with me from the first spark of an idea to the final full stop: thank you. To my parents, Benter Apiyo and Paul Kowino, your belief in me has been my greatest asset. To my siblings, Stephen, Elvince, Nelson, and Mary Faith, your encouragement and patience during the long hours of writing meant more than you know.

I must also extend my thanks to the team that turned this manuscript into a book. To my future agent and publisher, thank you for believing in this project. To the editors, designers, and proofreaders who polished this work, your skill and dedication have been invaluable.

Finally, to you, the reader. Thank you for joining me on this journey. My hope is that this book serves not as an ending, but as a beginning—a catalyst for conversation, action, and the change we so urgently need.

Appendix

This section is designed to serve as a bridge from reading to action. The ideas in this book are not just theories; they are calls to change our behavior, support effective work, and ground our arguments in established principles. Here you will find an action plan for allies, a directory of organizations on the front lines, and a summary of the foundational agreements that underpin the global fight for gender equality.

Appendix A: An Ally's Action Plan: A Toolkit for Men in the Workplace

Thank you for reading. If you are a man asking, "What can I do next?", you are already an essential part of the solution. Allyship is not a title you claim, but an action you take. Here is a practical toolkit to help you move from passive support to active change, starting on Monday morning.

The Meeting Audit: Create Space

In your next team meeting, don't just participate—observe. Track who speaks, who is interrupted, and whose ideas are ignored. Then, act.

Interrupt the Interrupter: If a female colleague is cut off, politely intervene. "Hold on, David, I'd like to hear the rest of what Mary was saying."

Create an Opening: Actively invite quieter voices into the conversation. "Sarah, you have a lot of experience in this area. What are your thoughts?"

Keep the Door Open: If you notice a conversation among male colleagues is dominating the time, deliberately open it up to others.

The Amplification Strategy: Give Credit

A common experience for women is having an idea ignored, only for a man to repeat it five minutes later to widespread praise. You can stop this.

Publicly Credit the Author: When a female colleague makes a key point, attribute it to her immediately and publicly. "That's a great insight. Building on Jane's point about supply chains..."

Second the Idea: If her idea is met with silence, be the one to validate it. "I agree with that. Let's explore that idea further." This gives it the traction it needs to be considered.

The Mentorship Mandate: Open Doors

Use your position and network to actively sponsor high-potential women.

Mentor and Sponsor: Mentorship is giving advice. Sponsorship is using your influence. Do both. Advocate for her promotion in rooms she isn't in. Recommend her for challenging, high-visibility projects.

Make the Introduction: Connect her with influential people in your network who can help her advance her career or business.

The Language Check: Challenge Bias

Bias is often hidden in our everyday language. Audit your own words and challenge those of others.

Avoid Coded Language: Don't call a woman "bossy" or "aggressive" for behavior you would praise as "assertive" or "confident" in a man. Don't describe women by their appearance when you describe men by their accomplishments.

Challenge Stereotypes: When you hear a biased comment or a sexist joke, don't stay silent. A simple, "What do you mean by that?" or "I don't find that funny" is often enough to disrupt the dynamic.

The Housework Audit: Start at Home

True allyship is not just a 9-to-5 job. The "double shift" is a primary barrier to women's professional advancement.

Make the Invisible Visible: Have a frank and honest conversation with your partner about the division of unpaid labor at home—the cleaning, cooking, childcare, and mental load of managing the household.

Aim for True Partnership: Actively take on your equal share of domestic responsibilities without being asked. When household and caregiving work is truly shared, it frees up women to compete on a level playing field outside the home.

Appendix B: Key Organizations on the Front Lines

This list is not exhaustive but represents a starting point for anyone looking to support or learn more from the organizations doing vital work across Africa.

For Girls' Education:

CAMFED (Campaign for Female Education): A pan-African movement that provides holistic support to girls in rural communities, from school fees and supplies to a powerful alumnae network.

Website: https://camfed.org

For Women's Economic Empowerment:

The African Women's Development Fund (AWDF): A Pan-African grant-making foundation that funds local, national, and regional women's rights organizations across the continent, supporting work in economic empowerment, political participation, and health.

Website: https://awdf.org

For Engaging Men and Boys:

Sonke Gender Justice: A South African-based organization with continental reach, Sonke works with men, boys, and community leaders to challenge patriarchal norms and combat gender-based violence.

Website: https://genderjustice.org.za

For Legal Rights and Justice:

TIMAP for Justice: An innovative organization in Sierra Leone that trains community-based paralegals to provide free, accessible justice services to the rural poor, empowering women to claim their legal rights.

Website: https://www.timapforjustice.org

For Women in Technology:

African Women in Tech (AWIT): A global network dedicated to supporting African women in the technology sector through mentorship, education, and networking opportunities to foster innovation and leadership.

Website: https://africanwomenintech.com

For Women in Business and Leadership:

New Faces New Voices (NFNV): A Pan-African network founded by Graça Machel, focused on expanding the role and influence of women in the financial sector.

Website: https://newfacesnewvoices.org

Appendix C: A Summary of Foundational Agreements

These key documents are pillars of the global and regional commitment to gender equality.

1. CEDAW (The Convention on the Elimination of All Forms of Discrimination Against Women)

Adopted by the UN in 1979, CEDAW is often described as the international bill of rights for women.

Core Principle: It defines discrimination against women and sets an agenda for national action to end it.

Key Mandates: It obligates signatory states to:

Incorporate the principle of equality in their legal systems and abolish all discriminatory laws.

Establish institutions to protect women against discrimination.

Ensure the elimination of acts of discrimination against women by persons, organizations, or enterprises.

2. The Maputo Protocol

Formally the "Protocol to the African Charter on Human and Peoples' Rights on the Rights of Women in Africa," it was adopted by the African Union in 2003. It is considered one of the most progressive human rights instruments in the world.

Core Principle: It supplements the African Charter by providing specific, comprehensive rights for women.

Key Innovations (going beyond CEDAW): It explicitly calls on states to:

Eliminate female genital mutilation (FGM) and other harmful practices.

Protect women's reproductive rights, including access to safe abortion in cases of sexual assault, rape, incest, and when the mother's health is at risk.

Ensure women's right to participate in political processes, including through affirmative action.

Protect the rights of vulnerable groups of women, including widows, elderly women, and women with disabilities.

3. Sustainable Development Goal 5 (SDG 5)

One of the 17 SDGs adopted by all UN Member States in 2015, with a target date of 2030.

Core Goal: "Achieve gender equality and empower all women and girls."

Key Targets (beyond the main goal):

5.1: End all forms of discrimination against all women and girls everywhere.

5.2: Eliminate all forms of violence against all women and girls, including trafficking and sexual exploitation.

5.3: Eliminate all harmful practices, such as child, early and forced marriage, and female genital mutilation.

5.4: Recognize and value unpaid care and domestic work through the provision of public services, infrastructure, and social protection policies.

5.5: Ensure women's full and effective participation and equal opportunities for leadership at all levels of decision-making.

5.6: Ensure universal access to sexual and reproductive health and reproductive rights.

Notes

This book is a work of narrative non-fiction, intended for a broad audience. While I have not used academic-style footnotes in the main text in order to maintain a fluid reading experience, the arguments and data presented here are built upon a foundation of rigorous research. This section is intended to acknowledge the key sources that informed each chapter and to provide a starting point for readers who wish to delve deeper.

Index

About the Author

Davidson Otieno Omondi is a dynamic researcher, community leader, and digital strategist dedicated to building a more equitable and sustainable Africa. As a student at Rongo University, he has distinguished himself through a remarkable commitment to leadership, serving as the Vice Chairperson of the Gender Club, the Chairperson of the Environment Club, and the Executive Coordinator for the Nurture Green Africa Foundation (NGAF).

His passion for leveraging technology for social good is evidenced by his work as the founder of Urban Pulse Kenya, a digital media platform, and his development of the Litein Comprehensive School website. These experiences have given him a unique, ground-level perspective on the intersection of education, technology, and community development.

Deeply informed by his upbringing across Kenya's Nyanza and Rift Valley regions, Davidson writes with a voice that bridges academic rigor with a profound understanding of the lived realities on the ground. The Unfinished Revolution is his debut book, a culmination of his tireless advocacy and a powerful call to action for his generation.

Find him online at:

www.urbanpulsekenya.co.ke

For inquiries, contact:

davidsonotienoomondi91@gmail.com

Don't miss out!

Visit the website below and you can sign up to receive emails whenever Davidson Omondi publishes a new book. There's no charge and no obligation.

https://books2read.com/r/B-A-LLJKE-AREUG

BOOKS 2 READ

Connecting independent readers to independent writers.

www.ingramcontent.com/pod-product-compliance
Lightning Source LLC
LaVergne TN
LVHW022117200926
848481LV00003B/1188